Your choice as a business owner, a professional network marketer, or a rising entrepreneur in any industry continues here!

Your Mind, Your Business
For the Rising Entrepreneur

Published by Skosha Divine Publishing

ISBN 978-1-7351902-8-0

A Workbook To Grow Your Business From Ideas To Manifestations

Your Mind, Your Business

For the Rising Entrepreneur

By Shanice S. DeTerville

A little message:

"When those who are "good" rest after a long day, the masters continue to burn the candle."

- Brian Carruthers, Building an Empire

Table of Contents

Introduction 7

One Pillar Towards Success 13

Cry for Your Why 25

Follow The Leader 31

Don't Sell, Make An Offer 35

Momentum 45

Object The Objections 49

Duplicate Yourself 55

Tell Your Story 59

Top 15 Books 67

Introduction

This workbook (the result of experience and a heart to give) is intended to shift your mind from feelings of being overwhelmed to a focused mindset. The purpose of this workbook is to give you insight and ignite a shift in your mind as you rise as an entrepreneur. This suggestive manual brings out the concept that in order to rise in business, you must first elevate your mind. This workbook has writing prompts to help encourage personal development as the main ingredient in the formula towards a successful business. If you are a business owner, use this workbook to reignite your drive towards your goals. If you are in network marketing, adopt these skills within your first 30 days and GO BIG!

If you are a teenager who aspires to be a kidprenuer, use this workbook to learn business concepts, skills and tips that give you a head start in winning big. In the content section, you will find topics that can be explored in sequence. Every subject will build on the other. Use the reflection page for free thoughts. If you write things down as ideas come to you (and they will come), you will have a secured space to return to. Use the guided questions to think outside of the box and get it all out of your head. Each question is designed to build on your larger vision bringing you closer to manifesting your ideas. The affirmations open up a different dynamic catered towards your success. Use your affirmations religiously, keep and repeat. Enjoy it, live it, and so it shall be.

Write 10x I am responsible for making things better in my life.

Reflect

Where ever you see your "Reflect" page is your time to have a creative space for free thoughts and notes.

Reflect

MY NAME IS NATASHA

I operate a small business in the fitness industry. I struggled with staying motivated because I do not always reach my financial goals. I decided to journal my journey anyways, and it's beginning to have a positive effect on my mindset. I read for 30 minutes a day and reflect on the lessons. Will you try it?

YOU CAN CALL ME PAUL

For 12 years, my wife and I have successfully run our family owned bakery, and now it's almost time to retire. One thing I wished I had done more than I had, is journaling my experiences along the way. We've had some ups and downs, and I'm sure our story would make a great book. Now, I write every day, so I don't forget a thing. Think about it!

#1 ONE VALUABLE

Pillar
Towards
Success is personal development practices

Highly Recommended

One Pillar Towards Success

Personal development is one of the most valuable pillars in business that an entrepreneur can commit to. This practice easily cultivates the mind and lunges you into a necessary shift that prepares you to obtain success. Whether a man is rich or poor in numbers doesn't equate to the state of his mind to be able to manage his own wellbeing.

Write where you are currently in your business journey and include where you want to go.
2-3 sentences

Continued... where you are currently in your business journey and include where you want to go. 2-3 sentences

Reflect

Methods to the Madness

30

Here's how it's done! Take 30 minutes daily and immerse yourself in personal development practices using your hearing, auditory, and visual learning styles.

- **Hear No Evil**
- **Speak No Evil**
- **See No Evil**

Hear No Evil

Listen to Wisdom

During the duration of your business, if you take time to listen to healing words, high vibrational sounds such as beta waves, and positive affirmations, you will begin to attract more good business to yourself. This is Law!

Speak No Evil

Reading Improves Speech

Adding reading to your daily schedule will inevitably improve your vocabulary and speech. Pick up books from leaders in your industry who can provide you with tools and skills they've already obtained. This saves you time!

See No Evil

Look Within

We are in the digital era, and technology is King. Utilize your Televisions or smartphones to watch motivational speeches. Connect on social media with groups that serve with the purpose of increasing one's awareness. Have fun!

Reflect

CRY FOR YOUR WHY

Your WHY should be your heartbeat. It is the very reason you are doing business and the outcome if you take action or not.

What is your WHY?

Now that you have taken massive action and made your WHY tangible for you to see, you must commit to doing everything in your power to make this idea manifest.

WRITE THIS AFFIRMATION 10X

From ignorance, bring me truth.

Reflect

FOLLOW THE LEADER

until you adopt their leadership skills.

Who are the top players in your field and are they willing to be your mentor?

WHAT TYPE OF MENTEE WILL YOU BE?

Decide early what type of mentorship you want. Being mentored by someone can be easy for you, or you can get pushed.

Network to increase your net worth.

Reflect

DON'T SELL, MAKE AN OFFER

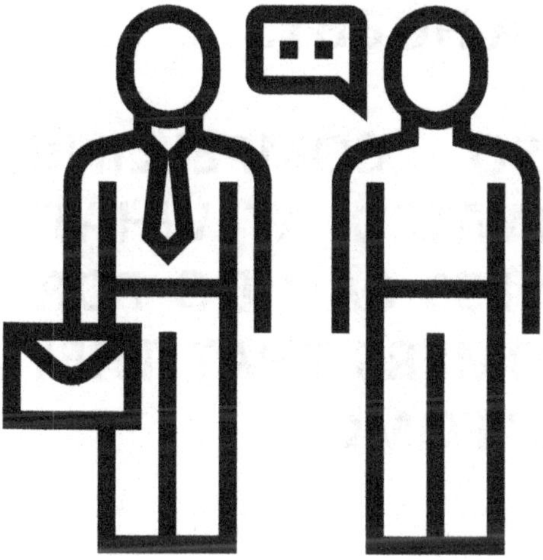

If you are doing good business, you will soon realize you are your brand, you are your products.

THE GOAL HERE IS TO EARN A LOT OF MONEY, IF YOU AREN'T EARNING MONEY THEN YOU HAVE A HOBBY.

BE SO COMPELLING, SO FASCINATED AT WHAT YOUR BUSINESS CAN DO FOR YOUR CUSTOMERS THAT THEY HAVE SOME "FOMO".

Fear of Missing Out on something specially designed for them is a consumer's nightmare. Make your customer feel special, each and every one of them.

SHARE YOUR

ELEVATOR PITCH

3 minutes is all it takes

First impressions are everything, and leaving a lasting impression is key. By now, your ideas have been written down, and you know where you want to take your business, and mastering this conversation piece will allow it to manifest.

You are meeting people through the law of attraction, and your elevator pitch is going to be your money maker.

IF YOUR BUSINESS IS YOUR PURPOSE,

THIS SMALL TALK ALONE SHOULD IGNITE A FIRE IN YOU.

FIRST AND FOREMOST

THE BEST WAY TO GET SOMEONE'S ATTENTION IS TO FIRST BE ATTENTIVE TO THEM AND FIND SOMETHING YOU LIKE.

Hey! I really love your smile.

Awe, thank you.

You are welcome. What type of work are you in that keeps you so happy?

Well, I am a barista at BUD's Tea, and you know we smile a lot. But I'm looking to start my own business. What about you?

Oh, Wow! You should definitely start your own business. I am the CEO of Life Goods. It's a growing company that invests in real estate on a global scale. We've helped 1000 millennials like yourself start their own businesses and retire young. We are looking to expand and could use a smile like yours for future markets. I will be glad to share my business card with you and set up a time to speak.

Reflect

Let's write your elevator pitch together.

An elevator pitch is a short announcement of what you do in business and how you do it.

I am ______________________________

____

We have helped ______________________

____

We plan to __________________________

____

We offer ____________________________

____

— Reflect —

MOMENTUM

THE SPEED OF THE LEADER IS THE SPEED OF THE TEAM.

Decide Now

How many employees or business partners do you want to have?

Do you need an LLC, S-Corp?

How much do you want to earn yearly?

How many hours a day will you commit to working on your business?

Do you need to invest in any course of marketing, management, etc.?

Reflect

OBJECT THE OBJECTIONS

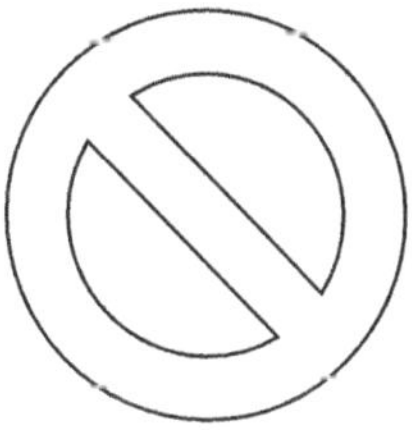

One ‘NO can lead you to the Yes that changes your life forever.

GO FOR THE NO!

Camman

OBJECTIONS

THERE IS
ALWAYS SOLUTION

O: The price is too high.

S: We have bundled options, so you will get more value for the same price

O: I am not located in your city.

S: We offer online service internationally.

O: I am not looking to buy anything today.

S: No problem. Will it be possible to send you an email about our services so you can look it over at a time convenient for you?

O: I don't have the finances to invest.

S: We can provide you with financial tips to help you make an investment that is suitable for your current situation.

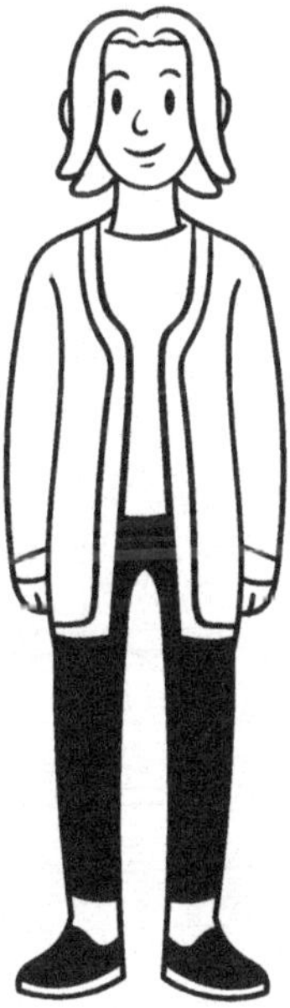

O: I don't have a computer at home.

S: No worries, our products are visible on any smartphone device.

Objections can lead you to exactly what you are looking for. Essentially you are a problem solver. Try it!

Write down some objections and find a solution.

More objections

DUPLICATE YOURSELF

INSPIRE OTHERS AND PASS THE TORCH.

Can you teach someone what you know?

Are you an influential person?

Do you want to make a difference in someone's life?

Answer these questions below

Who are you?

Who do you want to be?

Reflect

TELL YOUR STORY

Here is how you can choose which story to tell.

What makes a good story?

YOUR WINS!

BRUTAL HONESTY!

BEFORE & AFTER!

ADVENTURE!

FEAR OF MISSING OUT!

FEAR AND DESIRE!

ANYTHING THAT
CREATES AN EMOTIONAL HIGH.

S - SHARE THE SITUATION
T - TELL THE TASK AT HAND
A - ACTIONS NEEDED
R - RESULTS

USE THE STAR METHOD TO TELL YOUR STORY.

CHECK OUT THIS AN EXAMPLE OF ADVENTURE

Hi, I am Emily. I grew up in a pretty poor neighborhood. Every time, I would turn on the television I would always see rich kids doing some pretty cool stuff that I wanted to do. I decided when I turned 18 that I would pursue my dreams of becoming a fashion designer, so I can travel the world. Now that I'm 28, I own two franchises and have traveled to 23 countries, and I love my new lifestyle.

USE ONE OPTION FROM PAGE 59 AND DECIDE WHAT TYPE OF STORY YOU WANT TO TELL FIRST.

Reflect

Facts Tell and Stories Sell.

WHAT BOOKS ARE YOU READING

?

SERIOUS
QUESTION

HERE IS A LIST OF BOOKS TO ELEVATE YOUR BUSINESS & YOUR MIND

1. The One Minute Millionaire - Mark Hansen
2. The 4 - Hour Work Week - Tim Ferris
3. The Lazy Man's Guide To Richness - Joe Karbo
4. A Happy Pocket Full of Money - David Gikandi
5. You Are A Badass At Making Money - Jen Sincero
6. As A Man Thinketh - James Allen
7. The 21 Laws of Leadership - John Maxwell
8. Think and Grow Rich - Napoleon Hill
9. The Art of War - Sun Tzu
10. The Four Agreements - Don Miguel
11. The Secret - Rhonda Byrne
12. The Millionaire Next Door - Thomas J. Stanley
13. The Entitlement Cure - Dr. John Townsend
14. Breaking The Habit of Being Yourself - Joe Dispenza
15. God's Word Through Scriptures

**TO NOT KNOW IS BAD.
TO WISH TO NOT
KNOW IS EVEN WORSE**

-African Poverb

Reflect

Reflect

Made in the USA
Monee, IL
04 November 2026

67384435R00039